Teenage Angst

A Collection of Pain from the 90s

BEN SMITHFIELD

Heads or Tales Press
Copyright © 2016 Ben Smithfield
All rights reserved.
ISBN: 978-1-912704-31-6

DEDICATION

To

Good memories

Table of Contents

Acknowledgments I

As Soon As 1

Contamination 2

The Blue Angel (Be With Us) 4

He's No Different 5

Suzanne 6

Temporarily Gone 7

Chimes 8

Passover 9

Everything, and Including 10

Mr Machismo 11

Scrawny Girl vs. the Babe 12

Release.. 13

The Vegetable... 14

People Only Love You When You're Dead 15

A Pretty Good Day 18

Happy at Last 23

Death One 25

Death Two 26

Power of One, Now That You've Gone 27

Bye, Bye I'm Going to Mars 28

Slip Into a Dream 29

Sitting Here 31

Some… 32

Past of Bliss 33

The Snowflakes 35

Horses Are Calm 38

In the Eye 39

Our Votes For You 41

Reality Dreaming 43

Where Are We? 44

Maybe It's Gonna Be Alright 45

Flesh and Blood Part One …........................ 47

Flesh and Blood Part Two (Resurrection) ... 49

Flesh and Blood Part Three (All) 51

Flesh and Blood Part Four (The Contemplation) ... 52

Flesh and Blood Part Five (The Ice Age) 53

Flesh and Blood Part Six (Comprehension) 54

Flesh and Blood Part Seven (Rest for All) 56

2125AD 57

For You 60

The Face of Light, Gone 61

Every Night, You Rise 62

To a Loved One 63

Now's the Time 64

Be My Friend?	65
Getting Older	66
Sometimes	67
Where the Road Leads	68
In 2 Deep	70
Through a Window: Back and Forth	71
When?	72
Rolling Glass	73
The Mask	75
What's Inside?	76
I'm in Hell, (Won't Someone Help Me?)	78
Stages	80
Discovery?	81
The Realisation	82
The Everyday Pain	84
I'm Here	86

ACKNOWLEDGMENTS

Cover designed by Reimarie Cabalu

As Soon As

As soon as you're born you start dying,
Never any truth always lying.
As soon as you touch you start to see,
That all around is pain and misery.

As soon as you learn you start to realise,
That all you're being taught are lies.
As soon as you listen you start to think,
That they'll get you as soon as you blink.

As soon as you try you start to cry,
That you can never reach that all time high.
As soon as you run they see your tracks,
You know you can never relax.

As soon as you dream they're in your thoughts,
Even up there you can be caught.
As soon as you scream you're not heard,
They won't even come when your emotions stirred.

As soon as you wave no one responds,
You weren't that popular for too long.
As soon as you leave you're out the door,
No one cares about you anymore.

Contamination

The birth of a child
That grows in pain
The wife of a man
That showers in vain.

The experience of pleasure
That was most hated
The irony of time
That is most fated.

The worrying of the future
That transcends from detest of the past
The unhappy situation
That will forever last.

The hidden truths
That protects you all
The painful cover-up
That keeps the guilty to rule.

The daily soul destroying
That eats inside
The betrayal of family
That your face fails to hide.

The one forced night
That replays in your mind
The future certificate
That's already been signed.

The butcher walks on
That you set free

Teenage Angst

The life is over
That he decreed.

The Blue Angel
(Be With Us)

The angel of blue with warmth in her face,
Shudders over with a smiling embrace.
Helping forget the innocence of youth,
Lighting up the forbidden truth.

Making all seem a dream,
Surrounding us with a silent screen.
Securing the importance that's inside,
Giving us all a tremendous pride.

Holding up the hardest goodbye,
The golden tears sweeter than our frightened cries.
In her our belief,
Laying to rest the others with a papered reef.

He's No Different

The man comes out frightened and scared
People look, a long hard stare.
He's natural as from birth
People point, 'Look at his girth!'
He's wearing clothes people still see through
Because he's overweight people choose to.
They look upon him with disgust
Yet they can't believe, they're all aghast.
Society classes him as obese
He's a snail moving on grease.
They all accuse he's a scrounger
Thinking he sits all day on his lounger.
Who's to say what's big and small?
Watch your mouth please don't call
Walk right past there's nothing worth seeing
He's like you and me - a human being.

Suzanne

Suzanne's a working class girl
To you and I she's in a different world.
Doesn't work nine to five,
Working unsociable hours to stay alive.
Sold out when she was thirteen
Got tangled up with a dirty old fiend.
Eight years on she's still on the street
After all she has to eat.
Suzanne's a person with a non-existent pride
Somebody who has nothing to hide.
Has no dreams, she doesn't know how to
Just wishes she could be someone new.
Charges very little, gives away all
When she does make her pimp will call.
She dresses always nearly half-naked
Believes every night that one day she'll make it.
Suzanne has no control over her life or mind
The pimp sees to that with drugs and anything else he'll find.
He's her influence and voice
And while he's around she has no choice.
Perhaps one day Suzanne will break free
She deserves a normal life, don't you agree?

Temporarily Gone

His mind spun off
And left the Earth
Leaving behind his tears.

He was gone
Felt he won
Up to the blazing sun.

Soon he melted
Tears all dried
As he floated back to Earth.

His mind stuck on
As the spirit rose
Fully recovered from the overdose.

Chimes

Murderous vibes
Spilt off edges
Onto children's toes

But what we become
When we meet
Our carnivorous foes

The tides will turn
Taking away
The excess of our lives

And what we perceive
As burning candles
Will stick into us like knives

Passover

He wandered in from the cold
And told me his soul had just been sold

He struggled over to a wooden chair
To catch a scarce breath of air

He rubbed his hands and then his feet
To charm back the deserted heat

He fished out some money and bought a drink
Needing something to help him think

He threw up his hands to his head
And prayed that he wished that he was dead

He stood up and let out a vile scream
Then downed a double with ice Jim Beam

He dusted down his clothes and strolled over to me
Touching my shoulder he whispered in glee

He walked back out into the cold
After telling me my soul had just been sold

Everything, and Including

Grey days, winter blues
So washed up and used.
Rainy haze, summer days
Wake up in a fiery blaze.

Tricolour moon, Mr Doom
Gonna rise up soon.
Crazy heat, smiling sun
When all is said and...

Blasé scene, a Mrs Greene
Feel so fresh and clean.
Cascading sky, no god answers why
Dreaming of saying a final goodbye.

Mr Machismo

Mr Machismo is a greying man,
A greying man with a fake suntan.
A man who'll wear black sunglasses anytime of year,
Black sunglasses to match the rest of his gear.
He'll pile on the gel and pull back his hair,
His hair so slick it'll bring the birds to his lair.
A guy whose tastes in clothes is beyond compare,
Clothes so designer, no expense spared.
He owns a sports car so flash,
A sports car that must've cost a lot of cash.
And here he is now just to say hello,
Look at him stroll over, he is so mellow.
Well, Mr Machismo, I wish you the best of luck
"Aye that's good of ya, thanks chuck."

Scrawny Girl vs. the Babe

The Scrawny Girl lays down by the glistening pool
Her fragile insignificant bony figure a blemish in the sunlight
The cheap bikini that hangs on her loosely
That hangs on her pale sun-deprived skin
Her adolescent years show with her puny barely visual breasts
The long tattered brown ragdoll hair clings to her head
She sits up and rubs factor triple digits cream into her bones
As she turns she sees the Babe glide towards her
The Babe, a tanned blonde with a figure like Helen, lays next to her
The sun shimmers on her body and bounces off to her side
Rays of light sparkle in her Diana eyes
The Babe smiles and a flash of white light strikes
Her ample breasts that erect and her perfectly curved hips that draw
A designer bikini to hide/show off her body, to tease and tempt
Smooth body, waxed beautifully, hair that sways with the gentlest of breezes
Her model body artists devour to depict
The Scrawny Girl looks on, staring at the Babe
Jealousy flows over the Scrawny Girl onto the Babe like wind on a car in a tunnel
The Babe is unaffected, she's as pure as Chinese baby formula and above us all
An eternity above Scrawny Girl and will always be

Release

She wakes up
Another bad night - the final one
Has a bath
Now she's Ariel fresh
Cuts her long hair – surgery short
Writes a note to say, 'Thank you'

Scours the bath
Lies down inside naked
Takes a sharp Japanese steel
Along the vein slits her wrists
Blood is free and is allowed to rush
Free flow of liquid and the escaping sound of relief

Life drains
Peace is replenished
Stillness may rule the physical
But the spirit moves
Gone is the pain
And life for us is still the same

Goodbye

The Vegetable

Dried up wrinkled old man
Lost all his hair,
Blind as a bat
Stuck in a chair.

Hearing aid out of batteries
Voice box on the blink,
Memory all in pieces
Mashed up mind unable to think.

Eyes stare aimlessly
Trickle of saliva flows,
Heart beats slowly
Cancerous cells grow.

Arm hooked up by a drip
Machines pump his air,
Bladder connects to a bag
Chaplain wastes time on prayer.

Nothing to live for
Staying alive makes him crazier,
He wants it all to end
His only hope is euthanasia.

Please grant it.

People Only Love You When You're Dead

Throughout your life

No one cares
No one phones
No one's there

They'll just choose

To use
To lose
To abuse you

So that when you're down

They'll kick
They'll trick
They'll pick you up & pull you down

Because no one loves you

Not a single   Mother Teresa
                                      Pope John Paul
                                      Princess Diana
                                      Loveable fool

Until

Darkness inhabits your day
Winter comes in the middle of May
Your heart stops breathing

And you're no longer gratefully living

Then

Enter the first day of rest
Enemies come to pay their best
Weeping silently, loudly shedding their tears
Covering up their private cheers

Memorials, ceremonies, wide spread grief
In the ground your angered soul seethes

A curse on you all from the unloved jewel!

Worship me, praise me
Lavish attention on me
Build me up to a god
Talk about me with smiles
Dedicate songs to me
Give me those awards
Create a lifelike statue
Name theatres after me
Have flowers in my memory
Use my name, milk it to death
Earn your money through merchandise
Write about me with affection & how great I am
Make pilgrimages to my home
Hold lookalike contests
Have yearly anniversaries
Hold candle lit vigils
Say prayers with me in mind
Name your children after me
Stick me up on your wall
Use me for advertising

Teenage Angst

    Put me up on a pedestal
    Cry when you hear my name

But above all

        Cherish me
        Want me
        Need me
        Love me
    Now that I'm dead

A Pretty Good Day

Today's going to be a good day
I'm going to wake up bright and early
And go for a run
Yes, burn those unwanted calories
Lose weight must lose weight
Been told many times,
"Have you put on weight since I last saw you?"
Fit into jeans
Today's going to be a good day

Today's going to be a good day
I'm going to come back from the run…
Slimmer
Dripping with sweat
Mm, see that weight stream away
Have a shower
Nice cool shower and get clean
Smell real nice – for the ladies
They like that
French after-shave and brand name gel
Looking good
Today's going to be a good day

Today's going to be a good day
Go to a café for breakfast
Have a nice tall glass of freshly squeezed OJ
Toast with shredless marmalade
And a warm blueberry muffin
Tastes good and relatively healthy too
Health is important if you want to live longer
And who doesn't want that?
Today's going to be a good day

Teenage Angst

Today's going to be a good day
Buy an intellectual newspaper
Information is necessary
Keep informed of latest news
So we know all about you
Go home and watch people with aid of TV
We're so lonely
'I sleep with my family and have sex with my pets'
Today's going to be a good day

Today's going to be a good day
Meet friend and socialise
Share a chat and have a coffee
Need caffeine
Need spoken words
Such intelligent conversation
Philosophise about nothing
We know all
We – Know – All
Today's is going to be a good day

Today's going to be a good day
Organise schedule and plan future holiday
Busy days ahead
Want a break, live within the walls of freedom
Must clear… pay the bills
Everything absorbed… can again relax
Relax – remember the song
Will do it
Today's going to be a good day

Today's going to be a good day
Buy fresh flowers and lay them

In memory…
Go for appetising meal
Mm fresh food in the open air
Leave a tip – no one else will
'Turn around and look at your life
Then move a hundred steps"
Stroll to the park and inhale
Glance up at the sun and tan
Lift your arms – feel good
Today's going to be a good day

Today's going to be a good day
Refresh the home
Clean thoroughly, rid the germs
Hoover, spray, wipe and smile
Like new
All's in place within home and mind
Today's going to be a good day

Today's going to be a good day
Buy champagne – the best of course
That'll impress her
Set it up in a bucket of ice
Along with unlighted candle, and
Man made rose
Picture perfect – now just one more thing
The girl
Today's going to be a good day

Today's going to be a good day
Drive along popular road
Keep going till I spot her
Found her waiting patiently
Alone, ushering away another car

She's a light in the dark
In black – perfect
A blooming rose among the urban decay
Approach her invite her, take her
Today's going to be a good day

Today's going to be a good day
Share a glass of champagne
And share a brief conversation
Pay compliment
She's eager for me
Seduces me to the bedroom
Undresses me feel her breath
Tingles… soothes
We screw deeply, wet where it matters
Exultation, exhilaration
Worth…
Today's going to be a good day

Today's going to be a good day
Alone, now can cleanse of physical and spiritual dirt
Reminder on sheet
So content except feel primitive
Cut, shave born again
Almost time
Pull out closed drawer and take out piece
Place it by where I shall leave
Vermin hungry, they need me
Release the lovers into the freedom of apartment
Today's going to be a good day

Today's going to be a good day
Busy times ahead
Sit back, and relax against favoured wall

By my friend double 'M'
Caress him… Touch, lick excretion zone
And pull…
Explosion of dormant volcano
Waterfalls
Hell thrives in carpet
Food for thought and for the lovers
Dinner over moonlight
Buffet – all you can eat
The finest red meat
Chew the conjoined worms gurgle the wine
Lovers take your time and enjoy
For today is a good day

Happy at Last

It was dead.
The black furry creature was dead.
Tom had stared at it for half an hour
It hadn't moved.
Movement was a sign of life,
It must be dead.
Tom had seen some life
But they were miniature worms,
Miniature worms that had ingratiated themselves with it

Tom stood still and kept staring.
Flies were now buzzing around
Attracted by the deathly stench given off by the foul creature.
It was now getting dark and the garden took on a new atmosphere
An atmosphere of a cemetery
Except Tom felt no peace here
All Tom could see hear and smell was death
The death of an arrogant, lazy creature
A creature that deserved to die

Tom smiled
He was sure it had passed on
All it was now was food and a home for the disgusting
Tom examined the creature more closely
Dents, blood and brain were visible
Tom was pleased
The shovel that lay beside it had done its job
Now Tom had to rid the creature from his sight
And then he could feel at ease

Five long years the creature had tormented Tom
Now the torment was over
Victory was his
Everybody would be pleased with Tom
Tom had done a good job
The evil creature was now gone
Tom felt at peace
"It's dead," Tom enthused

Death I

Shell of a human being
Things that aren't worth seeing.
Insides of someone's heart
Too difficult to part.

Spirit of a human corpse
Never distinguished, can't distort
Fleeing to the sky, waving a goodbye
Leaving behind loved ones when you die.

Death II

An indignity being buried six feet underground,
Why not just toss you on top of a mound?
Smells appear, decay sets in
You spirits thankful you never sinned.

After all that work and graft, what was the point?
You'll always end up in this joint.
After all those meals you're now the main course,
You have no choice you're just a corpse.

Power of One, Now That You've Gone

Death is coming round to you
What can you do?
A lifetime's load of pain and suffering
Thrown on top of you.
What a way to go!

Under a cloud of darkness
No light was shed,
Might as well be blind!
Everyone's favourite little Miss Creeper
Hand in hand with the Grim Reaper.

In the middle of confusion
You're lost in the way
Where are you now?
Hope you're in paradise you deserve to be
Always looking out for me, me, me, me.

Death came and went
(What's done isn't done?)
You're now out of the picture
Your face no longer a regular fixture

Glad you're gone
Power of one

Bye, Bye I'm Going to Mars

This Earth is falling to pieces
Society going to crumbs
It's true I'm feeling high right now
So I'm off to see me mum.

This England is getting too cold right now
And everywhere else is blurred,
I tried it in Turkey one time
And managed to get off with a Kurd.

This old town ain't what it used to be
It's lost all its panache,
I hope my life will be different up there
Where I'll be free to smoke my stash.

This lonely flat is killing my head
Too small, I feel confined
I'll have a lot more space soon
To rest my weary drugged out mind.

Slip into a Dream

Fall into bed
Slip into a dream.
You're in your world
Yes you are King
...And she's your Queen.

Brown turtles are your servants
Jokers are your friends.
Pink is the colour of water
Sky is always bright
...And there's no night.

Main course: Cookies and cream
Chocolate milk champagne
Grass is always green
Tobacco dead cheap
...And you're still asleep.

Gold and silver grows on trees
Money made from leaves.
People sex is free
Women with three breasts
...And there's no time to rest.

Clothes keep clean
You eat off the floor
No doors.
Everything always open
...And your eyes are closed.

Swear compulsively
You stink of drink

Your mind starts to think.
You awake but your body's oozing
...And you're still snoozing.

Sitting Here

Sitting here, door open, alone in my room
Writing down feelings, feeling the cool breeze
Listening to skin tingling music and puffing away
Sipping a steaming drink, mixing it with a Russian creation
Floating body and mind, hairs on end
Catching ideas like butterflies in my long ear
Mind drifts off sifting thru grass
Call out someone's name from the recent past
The speaker next to me plays a guitar riff
Spine goes ice cold, roll another spliff
Still sitting here, the breeze runs thru my hair
Writing down more feelings I have without a care

Some...

Somebody I know with a Versace scent
Someone I fell for as I was meant
Something between us that we all know as love
Somehow it found us like a Prince dove
Somewhere to go to be with you
Sometime soon so I'm not without you

Past of Bliss

Lonely here without you
No medicine for this.
All there is
Is this past of bliss.

Rising from bed
Declining smiles
Look around
Can't see you for miles.

Catalogue memory
Covered in tears
Happiness was there
But far from here.

Lonely here without you
No medicine for this,
All there is
Is this past of bliss.

Stay within, far from her
This cannot be…
Arms wrapped
Struggling free.

Melt the bar
The heart goes too
Keep it back
It tries for you.

Lonely here without you
No medicine for this

All there is
Is this past of bliss

The Snowflakes

Crystal, with a hint of white
Snowflakes
Drifting lazily, helplessly falling
To the ground
Upon touch melting, turning to transparent water
Drawn like magnets
They form together, a wall of ice
So cold
Yet so fresh and strong, jealousy presides
Over me
They are one, always together
Forever growing
Joined by whiter stronger flakes
A velvet white coat of arms
The sky throws down more ammunition
A vision of white
Pelting the ground with a barrage of attacks
The victim caves in
Covered with layer upon layer of snow
Earth's suffocated
Still the flakes soldier on, covering more
Until all is white
Yet the skies shed more, a factory production line of snow
Heavier and thicker
Like clay they form into interesting shapes
Soft and smooth
They now fall into and create giant men
Sinister looking
Though the snow has created happiness for the child
Happiness craved by me
It's taken a stranglehold on our land

Keeps a tight grip
Now they think they've won, completing their mission
Mr Frost is laughing
At us and our feeble attempts to rid him of our country
Still he eerily laughs
But things are changing, the skies production line grinds to a halt
Jacks cries can now be heard
All around, as the last few snowflakes fall to the ground
Falling to their inevitable death
They know it, the flakes try to reverse their fall but they can't
They'll all perish
Those pellets that hit the ground now fall like cotton wool
Soft and pleasant
The wall of ice breaks and melts
Refreshing the Earth
Giving its life back and releasing its grip
White now back into colour
Colour that's shown up by the sun
And the sun shines on me
And those crystal snowflakes, as they melt away
Slowly dying
No longer attracted to each other, they go their separate ways
Till they meet again
When they'll be replenished and full of life
Back to haunt me
And the Earth, who's the victim, will die again
The land will change
Old green hills into miniature Alps
But for now the grass grows
Flowers will bear their fruit and trees will breathe life

Teenage Angst

Until winter arrives
Bringing with it those delicate white harmless snowflakes

Horses Are Calm

Daylight leaves
Shadows are cast over the land
Horses are calm
Fallen leaves dance in the growing wind
Darkness resurrected
Horses are calm
Grass sways together like a flock of birds
Trying to avoid the newly arrived rain
Horses are calm
The wooden stable creaks and aches
Branches on trees try to hang on
Horses are calm
The barn door smacks open and closed
Hay and dirt mingle before taking flight
Horses are calm
Ferocious wind swirls round battering all
Upending roots causing plants and trees to collapse
Horses are calm
Roofs lift off launching into space
Ground is dug up leaving gravely holes
Horses are calm
Glass is shattered
All around disintegration
Horses are calm

In the Eye

They're performing in the circus
Attracting the spies of broken rules
Throwing around a merry dance
Proving they are fools.

Above the moons shadow
In and out of the crooked fence
They juggle with all they hold
Within the secure broken tents.

But they know what circles
Around the game they play
The die that counts to four
Turns a joke on pray.

Without a listen they see what they do
Accepting slaps on backs
Hands laid out not caring
As witnesses fall through cracks.

With their pretty little lives
Always wearing a shirt and tie
Just because their heads are held high
It doesn't mean they can't lie.

Pounds slip through pockets
Into foreign arms
Visibly not being caught
But they can't hide behind their charms.

And they perform in a circus
Feeding us with lies when we demand

Walking the tightrope with skill
Brushing us away with that laid out hand.

Stand

Our Votes for You

My vote goes to you, Right Honourable Government Minister.
Waste all our money decorate your flat
Forget the homeless perm your black and white cat.

My vote goes to you, Right Honourable Government Minister.
Bring all the worlds nuclear waste here
Radiate us and we'll all cheer.

My vote goes to you, Right Honourable Government Minister.
Increase the taxes treat your friends
Don't worry about those living near the end.

My vote goes to you, Right Honourable Government Minister.
Kill the health service make us wait
Let us succumb to our inevitable fate.

My vote goes to you, Right Honourable Government Minister.
Give yourself a hefty rise you've worked so hard
Ignore the poor shivering child who's starved.

My vote goes to you, Right Honourable Government Minister.
Don't give in to equal rights
Make sure your rented boy is home by twilight.

My vote goes to you, Right Honourable Government Minister.

Accept all bribes you need the money
To keep your wife in shoes and roses to your honey

My vote goes to you, Right Honourable Government Minister.
Spend half your year in Saint-Tropez
We love working for minimum pay.

My vote goes to you, Right Honourable Government Minister.
Your seat without doubt is so deserved
Every vote won truly earned.

Reality Dreaming

Starship children come into my dreams
Marshmallow men who seem to be free
Flowers on the ocean, submarines on the Earth
Alcopop babies telling us what it's worth

Snowmen warming up in the morning sun
Sunny evenings are here to come
Cold summer days with wilting trees
Winter days with warm summer breeze

Is this reality or am I just dreaming?
Does this life have any meaning?
Is dreaming the best it can be
or is dreaming reality?

Snow and icebergs disappeared
Take a look and see what we feared
What's gonna happen if we stay
Starship plane please take me away

Is this reality or I just dreaming?
Does this life have any meaning?
Is dreaming the best it can be
or is dreaming reality?

Where Are We?

We float on high
On our little islands
Segregated by all we know
Being pulled via chain
Closer, closer

We share the energy
That is us
Manipulated and decimated
Where do our beliefs lay?
Anywhere, nowhere

We reason with each other
Not knowing what they know
In control in our imaginations
We're slipping further away
Beyond help, beyond

We walk alone oblivious
Crying out for comfort
Seeking a better
When do we stop?
One day, not today

Maybe It's Gonna Be Alright

We may have uncontrollable leaders
Who wish to interfere,
Destroying all in their path
Causing mass deaths each year.

We may have fame-seeking Governments
Citing peace as their objective,
As long as they're remembered in history
And their missiles are effective.

But...
          Maybe it's gonna be alright
        Perhaps the world will see the light

We may have a suicidal world
That wants to press self-destruct,
A place that can't seem to settle
An Earth that looks truly fucked.

We may have a power-hungry people
Where nothing seems to satisfy,
Even when we have comfortable lives
All we really do is die.

But...
          Maybe it's gonna be alright
  Perhaps the world will climb out of this deep plight

We may have an Earth on its eighth life
With once flourishing wildlife,
Forests full of trees burning
And rivers' neck to a knife.

We may have starving countries
Buying arms from the superior West,
But as long as tills keep ringing
Who cares about the rest?

But...
>Maybe it's gonna be alright
>Perhaps the world will regain its sight

We may have great weapons
That can destroy thousands of miles away,
Yet we can't cure age long diseases
That will not keep at bay.

We may have fantastic ideals
Of where we all get along,
But as long as we see race, creed, religion
Human beings can never be strong.

But...
>Maybe it's gonna be alright
>Perhaps the world will give up the fight

Flesh and Blood Part I

I was created from where everybody stands
I am the earth that you sow
The water that you drink
The spark from the fire that burns in you all

I was born north, south, east and west
I'm the direction you go to
The magnet that attracts you
The path that leads to your final destination

I was from the sea to the ground to the air
I am everywhere
The reflection in the mirror
The picture in the frame

I was raised in the fields that don't age
I'm gazing over the stars
The ones that populate your eyes
The make up of your destiny

I was the seed of your labour
I am the cause you live for
The revolution you seek
The answers don't find
I was the breeze that turned into wind
I'm the power behind your mind
The images you dream
The thoughts you can't contain

I was the key that couldn't unlock doors
I am the invisible barrier
The peace you look towards

A Collection of Pain from the 90s

The tissue that can't quench your tears

I was the making of your doing
I am the supreme protector
The one you name you fight your fight for
The encouragement of decline

I was I am
The bread and wine
The flesh and blood
The eternal shrine

Flesh and Blood Part II (Resurrection)

Spilt blood onto my Earth
Shattering of bone
Power and wealth
Creation and destruction
Wrath of love folded arms
A descending calm

The shrine the shrine
The blood the wine
Tears
Tears that seep into wounds
From wounds from eyes
From bastards' lies
The children cry

Caucasian persuasion
Blackening reaction
Flooded fields
Poor man yields
To the clouded skies
I see doves die

A miner's gold
A lover's hold
The falsity the pomposity
The falls and rise
The flowers cries

A blackening

Charcoal dust
Avenging lust
Angels pry shower with wings
Guardians and me

The bread and wine
Impending flood
Crash and shine
Kiss your shrine

Slither and slather
Wallow in demise
Whilst I rise

Flesh and Blood Part III (All)

I've climbed the deepest ocean
I've scaled the setting sun
I am the whole world
Rolled into one

I've weathered the strongest storm
Survived the bleakest rain
Crossed those separate paths
Which derive from the harshest pain

I've wallowed in the lowest depths
Hidden in metaphors
Fallen through trouble
Onto empty floors

And now:

I am here naked
Yours for the world to see
Please make use of me
Please make use of me
Please make use of me

Burn me burn me
Lynch me kill me
Fuck me kiss me
Praise me hate me
Love me… love me

Fly and free
Consider me be

Flesh and Blood Part IV
(The Contemplation)

Consider
The World an orange
Take a bite
And suck it dry
For this is what you do
Hurting, hurting me

I'm the core
The source
Consider a moment
A day
The light burning into
Disarray

Joy for the World
Or for a Pound
Capitalist corruption &
Communist destruction or vice-versa
Just for a tear
A smile, a piece of flesh
Drip dry
And fucking crucify

Flesh and Blood Part V
(The Ice Age)

Into ice
The people turn
As all things die
Inside
If anybody was there
In this frozen universe
Nothing can matter
To what you instigate
For your concern
We worry

I'll open the clouds
You see the light
A brief respite
For the fury and anger
And the fire that'll rain
Melt you and seize you
Capitulate and decimate
But I'll be here above you
Having risen observing rapid decline
Wasting away in seconds

Screaming, the shrieks
The wailing
Nothing to ponder
Wistfully smile and look the other way
Is this bliss?

Flesh and Blood Part VI (Comprehension)

Bliss?
A crusaders blind mist

An encroaching war
A lover's monologue lore
Feeding into a maggot infested gape
Everybody into rape

With the eternal genocide of the world
Love of death – reasoning will to survive
Split the head open
& Discover the lie

(Peel the scalp, the cranium
Unleash the worms
Slice with a carving knife – pink
A small ocean – waves – draining fluid
Beauty of the decadence of man
As a can opener on a tin
Access)

Lover's love
Educating bath
Educating what?
Nothing learned
Or realised
A time to go
In the line with the crow

A cycle?

Teenage Angst

Beyond the life
You get thrust into the blade of the knife

Flesh and Blood Part VII
(Rest for All)

I will hide
Then show
And destroy what I created
I am all-powerful
I will flood the fields with blood
Shower the towns with pain
I will create again – beauty in havoc
Misery
Stop all generations
End the travesty
Bow to your saviour
And worship your shrine

2125 AD

What's it gonna be like soon,
When people live on the moon.
Space travelling like riding a bus,
Things you can't comprehend will be a must.

Go back in time,
To get a new, now vintage wine.
Place your cash on a sure thing,
You know you're gonna win.

Freeze dried food old but new,
Drinks that you can chew.
Whole meals in just one pill,
Quick and easy able to fill.

Go out to play when you're still inside,
Bulging fat that you're able to hide.
The rush of a drug that you haven't taken,
Experience orgasm with love you're not making.

When interracial love is history,
And intergalactic love is the current story.
Babies half human mixed with some other,
When a baby's father is its mother.

Everything you need is at home,
If you go out you'll surely be alone.
No crime, big brother's watching you
Everyone's a criminal, what can you do?

New and more effective diseases in circulation,
Easier to rid people of a nation.

A Collection of Pain from the 90s

Health dictates the all year round fashion,
A silver space suit to dampen the passion.

No more roads because cars are flying,
Pollution's down governments still lying.
Transportation's easier through teleportation,
Quicker to get to your holiday destination.

Cities become all over metallic,
All workers are systematic.
Though workers are few and far between
Because most work is done by the machine.

All the worlds' monarchies overthrown,
Workers knocked down Millennium Dome.
Palaces are home to those without,
Societies suffer severe drought.

A republic for all nations,
Independence for a nation of Haitians.
Worlds' economy in terminal decline
The Chancellor says, 'Everything's fine'.

People fight for that last clean breath,
Secret organisations create a new Black Death.
Patients queue up, hospitals full,
It's okay there's a cure for 'all'.

People emigrating to Mars,
Earth's population decreasing fast.
Asteroid will soon destroy,
Media say it's a government ploy.

When the world starts to die,

Teenage Angst

People will have to forget about I, me, my,
Everything ceases to be live,
All this by 2125.

For You

Feelings departed when you left,
So many words were left unsaid.
The pain inside still here,
The pain we felt all those years.
Each day passing you become more distant,
A memory in the past that is hard to trace.
People we trusted who said were loved,
Were just there fooling us from the start.
Now you're gone, what's left to say?
We miss you, we love you, and we'll see you someday.

The Face of Light, Gone

The light in my life when darkness reigned,
Has been extinguished now that you've passed away.
The problems I have, I now face alone
The knowing face I turned to, gone, now one of the angels own.

Every Night, You Rise

I'd thought you'd gone
But still you rise,
In all my dreams
Right through my eyes.

And there you remain
A shadow in my mind,
Piece of history
That I constantly find.

A constant reminder
Of all things gone,
Moment of reflection
When things go wrong.

And the barriers that are placed
To help avoid you,
They all crumble
Just like I do.

So my eyes stay open
Every night of every day,
And I won't sleep
Till I find a way past May.

To a Loved One

Clouds dispersed, sky was clear
The heavens opened on your seventieth year.
Memories now past; time has flown
A future without you into the unknown.

With the shadow hung over gone
Now that the pain you suffered can't go on.
You're now free to sleep in peace,
And your spirit now at ease.

You left us for the final time,
Without any notice, without any sign.
Angels came and took you away,
When the sky was clear on a cloudless day.

Now's the Time

Looks like you might get back together,
It's been so long; it's now or never
A lot of time has sped right past,
If you see each other you'll catch up fast

A stupid row that caused a rift,
Left your relationship far adrift.
But despite the distance, you're always tied
By unequivocal love you can never hide.

When one of us walked on up to the sun,
Thought the three of us would now be one.
Alas the three of us became further apart,
Breaking our loved ones fragile heart.

Two became close and two steered clear,
No longer visibly holding each other dear.
Both of you showed too much pride,
Until you two in me confide.

We all know underneath the feelings there,
How much each of us really care.
If only the feelings had been shown,
It would've stopped breaking up our home.

We're now older, wiser too
Love bringing us together because we do,
A simple call will help mend
And make this fight come to an end.

Be My Friend?

Will you be my friend?
Be my friend until the dying end
The one who'll help if I'm in trouble
Heave me out of the collapsed rubble

Will you be my heart?
Be my heart when my body wants to depart
The one who'll keep me going all the time
Even when my clock starts to chime

Will you be my hands?
Be my hands when guiding me through the sands
The one who'll find me if I feel missing
Keep on looking when no one's listening

Will you be my eyes?
Be my eyes when mine are coloured with lies
The one who'll search if I see no truth
Believe in me when there is no proof

Will you be my friend?
Be my friend until my dying end
The one who'll help if I'm in trouble
Heave me out of the collapsed rubble

Getting Older

Another day lost, another day gained
God I wish I wasn't my age.
All those years I was so young
Now they've built up, formed, made me old
I feel like a piece of meat left unsold.

I used to be one of them now I'm not,
I'm sitting here watching as my body starts to rot.
My hair still here but for how long,
One day it'll turn to grey then be gone.

All things I see point to my age,
From the cardigans piled high in the wardrobe
To the slippers by the bed, with electric fire on red
Kettle always brewed, cupboard full of biscuits,
Spending my days on a puzzle trying to link it.

I wonder how old I'll be when I die,
The lines on my face tell no lie.
Sickness arriving, energy leaving,
In a permanent state of grieving.

Sometimes

Sometimes I think I'm a bird
Flying without wings
Sometimes I think I'm a cat
Living without the nine
Sometimes I think I'm a dolphin
Floating without fins
Sometimes I think I'm a bee
Buzzing without the honey
Sometimes I think I'm me
But I know that not to be true

Where the Road Leads

Seventeen years
And another few days
Beginning charades that have plagued my haze.

Echoes of past shroud my mind
Worrying future
It's the end of my time.

Speeding on the road ahead
People call
They won't stop till I'm dead.

But all I see
Are the glittering stars
Heaven knows if I'll make it that far.

All I know...
And all I can be:
Keep tripping on the life that is free

Still I'm plagued as I age
My mind, my time
And the haze that shines.

But I'll work it through
Open the eyes
And fight those fucking lies.

So whether I trip or speed along
This road I'm taking
This road
This road on the right

Teenage Angst

Away from confusion
Away from people
Away from the misery piled on us
The congestion, the suffocation
The grey

The choking smoke strangles life out of all the beings and doings and breathing becomes difficult, trapped in the centre, controlled by, used by those at the top.

Away... Away...

To the whispering blue ocean that calls my name...

In 2 Deep

I fall off into a subconscious sleep,
My mind goes off and into the deep.
Through spherical worlds and oblong shapes,
Into rivers filled with freshly crushed grapes.

Waking in a perilously warm ocean,
Rubbing myself with a cancer-ridden lotion.
Then serenely rising to the skies,
Getting my fill of staring eyes.

Tripping through Charlie's tunnel,
Separating the pure with my uncle's funnel.
Igniting the only thing that's good,
Accepting pleasure for my piece of wood.

Tucking into blue bottle pancakes,
Injecting milk with morphine to quell the aches.
Dressing up all in blue,
To match the suit that the skin gives you.

Climbing through lava lamps,
Reaching the end of excruciating cramps.
Rummaging amongst nightmares to try to escape,
Killing the mind that's been raped.

Hurtling off into a different speed,
Searching the one whom gives me need.
Leaving the life he gave me,
To meditate privately on my tree.

Here I sleep

Through a Window: Back and Forth

Look into a window
Empty as day
Vague sunlight I'm parched
Collapse across the room of the world
Lay the head down upon a pillow
Examination time:
'Loneliness is what follows
When the heart is set on love'
In through the door
When the window is closed
Clear and the words are obvious
Except when perceived as rude
And unwanted – me. I'm parched
Lying round the world
Out of the window into the universe
It's my face – expressionless
Upon a pillow – thoughts escape
Dreams occur, fail the exam
Back to loneliness

When?

When will the internal pain go away
And the external face show brighter days?
When will the happiness decide to come and stay
And the sadness inside go away?

When will my eyes become dry
And my mind stop trying to make me cry?
When will my aching heart stop hurting
And my wondering mind stop searching?

When will the sun shine on me
And my mouth turn up with glee?
When will my demons disappear
And the angels that left reappear?

When will I go in the right direction
And be free of any intrusion?
When will my life give me reason to live
And for me to know when to give?

Rolling Glass

Looking in the mirror
Seeing the dismantled figure
Cracked and jagged
Impossible to keep together

Pieces of you and I
Chewed up, spat out
Torn apart, crumpled up
Glued back together

And it rolls like glass
Shifting and changing divulging the past

A revealing, shameful reflection
Quicker than the shadow
Sprinkled with holes
All linked together

A shattering pane
A circumcised stain
Congealed and consoled
Folded away together

And it rolls like glass
Mutilated, forgotten memories, which last

Scattering of fragments
Sharp like skin and glistening blood layer the floor
Reflecting the passing images
Causing mass incisions together

Surmise the broken figure

Loaded is the pointed trigger
Ruined and burnt
Into floating ashes that fly - together

And it rolls like glass
Formulating, creating the all important mask

The Mask

Everyday I look in the mirror
See nothing
Nothing is there, just a mask
A mask of hate, of loathing.
I put my hand to my face
And feel the hard tired skin
I want to pick away all the
ills all the scabs that cover up the truth
The truth is that there is no/ne 1
Never in my crap life has there ever been truth
There has been death - plenty
And lies - bountiful
By people near me not close to me
But it's my lie for not exposing them
I should have shown up these untruths
Put things into the correct light
For all to see
Yes this face that I see everyday
is full of lies and hate and remorse
Remorse for being what I have become
The mirror tells no lies just the reflection
And the reflection shows nothing
For that is what I am
On the outside.

What's Inside?

Because no one understands
It's all an image
All a front
A complete and total lie

There is no …
Never has been for years
This is not me
But it's what I've become

Because no one understood
No one cared
A word or two does nothing
Commitment does - but where's that?

To be abandoned three times
By your 'loved' ones
There is no love
Only hate and it's mine

I own and control all the hate
I've had it for years
Building - layer by layer - brick by brick
Ignore the polite well-mannered boy

Manners generated by my mother
But where's she
Dead, killed by the worst
Being eaten alive then and now

There is no justice
No sense, no rationale

Teenage Angst

There is no understanding
For me the product of all that is not real

I'm In Hell, (Won't Someone Help Me?)

In a cage in my mind, in a cage all my life
Won't someone help me?
Stuck in these four walls, there's no way out
Won't someone help me?
Surrounded by layers of dead wood, dead
Won't someone help me?

A vision of hell so real
To live in a world that is surreal
A mind-blowing vision of fire
In a world that is so dire.

My hands were tied, throat lacerated
Won't someone help me?
Feet were cut, always go to ground
Won't someone help me?
Oppressed, depressed, suppressed – arrest!
Won't someone help me?

A vision of hell so real
To live in a world that is surreal
A mind-blowing vision of fire
In a world that is so dire.

Stages

So tired and so alone
Can't even be bothered to contact friends by phone
Just want to stay in bed
Relaxed and secure within my own head

Afraid of the outside
The sanctuary of home a place to hide
Can't cross the barrier of my front door
Even when the voice calling is yours

Feel caged and kept
I can't remember the last time I slept
Starting to constantly suffocate
Unable to properly defecate

By my side my Scotch friend
Helping to combat the cramps that will be my end
Though now not able to rid the pain
As pills drop down on me like rain

In the corner shaking
Every part of me hurting and aching
Can only think about ending me
And letting my destroyed spirit be

Discovery?

Black and white papers reveal everything
They know
Through visionary eyesight and psychic powers
They've seen through me
Years of wondering and self-examination
Has left me pondering
But the yearly adventure has come to a close
We are no longer in doubt
I have been judged and exposed
Let us all see and watch over
Look at me
Inspect every particle
Swallow any substance
Waver into any orifice
The diagnosis is set
The conclusions concluded
No trip from the doctor will be required
Give the final autopsy
Read out the prognosis
Consult no one
For the answer is known
Everything's declared
I have been laid bare
Strip me of all covers
And photograph the discovery that's been found
Print it, publish it - make it known
So the whole world (because they need to)
Can discuss and gossip
Can chat away in their little huddles
Talk about me, not care
For I am here for public consumption
Eat away and chew

Teenage Angst

Spit out and wipe
Then forget
I'm just another pawn in someone else's game
Now we all know
Who I was, am and will always be
…

The Realisation

I am unable to breathe
All I want to do is leave

Too much pressure piled on
Pressing against me so long

Squeezing out all I had to give
Causing me not to live

Haemorrhaging stress heaped on me
A weight so heavy can't be free

I can't escape and live my life
I cannot be nine to five

Don't want to be dictated to
Won't accept being told what I can or cannot do

Refuse to be trampled on
Won't listen to people who try and con

Going to keep my mind clean of influence
Steer clear of people who create malevolence

Will fight any demons
Never hear a preacher's sermon

Will only follow what my heart says
Won't be fooled by a temptress' caress

I am all that is pure
Not going to obey no hypocrite's law

Teenage Angst

Stay true to myself and relieve the weight
Learn to love all that I hate

Die and be born into a new life

The Everyday Pain

Burgundy blood trickles down through me
Proving the pain that I feel
How much longer can I sustain it?
As it becomes more unbearable by the day
So constant and consistent
Keeping to a tight schedule that ruins me
My life, my everyday existence
Creating worries that I do not need
So I suppress the enemy inside
Topping myself up with pills
Trying to control all my ills.
Why do I have to be the vulnerable one?
The one so susceptible to pain and illness
What have I done to deserve?

I want to rip this pain out
Claw my hand in and cleanse the inside
Emptying me of the demon
My soul needs peace, please

I cherish the soul but it's become demonic
Something that is controlled
Controlled by another life form
Not mine, but it's this that causes
pain and kills me inside
That causes excruciating cramps
And kills me

The burgundy blood still trickles down
Changing colour when it hits the water
Refreshed, it looks younger and brighter
Maybe the demons life is draining or

Maybe the replenished blood symbolises strength?
A growing strength inside me

What can it want from me?
I've given all I can - my life is all
The pain gets worse
And the blood still flows
It still exists as it stares up
At me, in my face
Playing with my eyes - a beautiful wine

Beauty in defecation
An apt ending

I Am Here

I am here
Alive
On this planet
The only one
The one

I am here
Alive
Alone on this Earth
No one else
No one

I am here
Alive
Above everybody
Because I see
I see

I am here
Alive
Purified by cleansing
Because I touch
I touch

I am here
Alive
Judging the puppets
Because I feel
I feel

I am here
Alive

Teenage Angst

Floating from you
I can elevate
I'm elevated

I am here
Alive
Juxtaposed with the population
I stand segregated
I'm on my own

I am here
Alive
Within the essence of freedom
Born with wings
I fly

I am here
Alive
The paragon of everything
I excel with ease
I'm already there

I am here
Alive
Preordained with fate
I lead my path
I'm near the end

I am here
Dying
On the final straight
I hear the chilled wind
I hear

I am here
Dying
Being called away
I know the clock is chiming
I know the time

I am here
Dying
Like a bee that's stung
The engine's stopped
I have no heart

I am here
Dying
Recording each breath
Treating them as contractions
I know it's getting nearer

I am here
Dying
Catching the last gasps of air
But I'm exhausted
I'm so tired

I am here
Dying
All things can seem divine
Skies so clear and blood's so fresh
I don't want to go

I am there
Dying
The light's so bright
Shining through my eyes

I'm seeing love...

...I am there

www.ingramcontent.com/pod-product-compliance
Lightning Source LLC
Chambersburg PA
CBHW021119080526
44587CB00010B/571